RECIPE FROM UPSIDE DOWN

FROM NETFLIX SERIES TV

NORRIE LEMON

This book is an unofficial guide
written by a Stranger Things fan.

The author, The publishers, or the book itself
are in any way associated with the program and its creators.

Stranger Things is a registered trademark of Netflix Studios LLC.

Norrie Lemon. Recipes from upside down (Italian Edition).
Wiks editions for Kindle Finished printing in July 2019.

Recipe Index

Recipe Index 3
Preface 1
SALATO 3
Mom's casserole 5
Crispy mini-meatballs 7
Meatloaf, green bean and mashed potatoes 9
Upsidedown Turkey with Coke 12
French Onion Barb 14
Divine French Fries 18
Scrambled Eggs 20
Spinaches with two cheeses sandwich 22
WAFFLE SALATI 25
Mini waffles cheeseburger 26
Eleven's Eggo Sandwiches 28
Bacon and chicken waffle sandwiches 31
Green slime waffle sandwich 36
Bacon, onion and mozzarella waffle sandwich 39
Eggo Waffle 41
Fried chicken, grilled cheese and pickled cherries sandwich 43
Bacon and Cheddar Waffle 47
Grilled cheese and fried chicken waffle 49
Bacon, Sriracha syrup and fried chicken waffles 52
Pizza Waffle 54
DOLCE 57
Ginger syrup 58
Pickled Cherries 60

- Nutella Cream 62
- Christmas Cupcakes 64
- Upsidedown Muffins 68
- Blood Drops Cake 71
- Chocolate Cake 73
- Apple juice cake 75
- Upsidedown Vanilla Cake 77
- Demogorgon Cake 80

WAFFLE DOLCI 83
- Strawberry ice cream and candies waffle sandwiches 84
- Demogorgon Sandwich 86
- Blueberries and peanut butter waffle sandwich 88
- Peanut butter and Jam Sandwich 91
- Rotted fruits Waffles 93
- Mud and worms Waffle 95
- Apple cider waffles 98
- Nuts and Pumpkin Waffles 100
- Chocolate and banana waffles 102
- Red Velvet Waffles 104
- Triple-Decker Eggo 106
- Pumpkin patch waffles 108
- Pineapple waffles 111
- Christmas lights waffles 113
- Lemon ice-cream and peanuts waffles 115
- Strawberry ice cream and rum waffles 117

COCKTAIL **119**
- Eggo my Eggo 120
- Upsidedown Cocktail 122
- Friends don't lie Cocktail 124
- Justice for Barb Cocktail 126
- Stranger Things Cocktail 128

Preface

Stranger Things is a Netflix series launched in 2016 and immediately acclaimed by critics. It has a horror-sci-fi mold, is set in the 1980s, and then takes us back in time.

We thought of paying tribute to the culture of those years by combining cooking with the old-fashioned science fiction culture, and this is how this collection of 50 recipes was born.

In the TV series, waffles, egg yolks, and many typical foods from the past are often mentioned. We have drawn inspiration from this by giving some of these a decidedly horror-themed tone, to others a Christmas look that recalls the Christmas lights, symbol of this TV series.

Stranger Things is synonymous with wonder, plot twists, friendship, risk and courage. This is why we wanted to experiment with decidedly stunning mixes. Some of these recipes are reminiscent of mum's lunch, others an evening with friends, others are suitable for a masquerade party.

Each of them has been specifically designed to recall Stranger Things, whether it is with a reference to a character or a particular episode. Towards the end you will also find recipes for unique and decidedly delicious cocktails!

We are sure that the lovers of this TV series will enjoy preparing these dishes, they will find them captivating to look at and tasty to savor.

We just have to wish you good fun and enjoy your meal!

We hope you enjoy our work, but above all that you like the recipes. We hope you enjoyed yourself, making this culinary journey set in the 1980s.

Thank you

SALATO

Mom's casserole

By now, everybody knows that Mrs Wheeler is a great cook and always succeeds in making the whole family happy with her recipes. During the episodes of the series, we have heard many dishes typical of the years '80 and one of these is the famous casserole. If we want to directly transport us in the houses of Stranger Things, let's put us to job and prepare the Mom's casserole.

Ingredients (x3/4 people):
- 3/4 potatoes
- 250 gs of cheese Cheddar
- 1 ounce of ham
- 6 onions
- 4 eggs
- Whipped cream
- 1 leek in pieces
- 1 pinch of salt
- 1 pinch of pepper

Preparation:
1. Start taking a pot and pouring water in. Make the potatoes boil and salt the water.
2. When they will be ready, drain them and peel them.
3. Now cut them to dice of average greatness.

4. Take a casserole now, in ceramics or crock, and introduce the potatoes in, with the ham and the leek.
5. Cut the cheese Cheddar to dices and the onions to thin slices, and then add them to the mixture.
6. Now take another bowl and beat the eggs inside, now add the whipped cream, the salt and the pepper.
7. Work the mixture with a ladle until it does become homogeneous.
8. After that, pour the dough above the ingredients inside the casserole.
9. Cover with plastic wrap and let it all to rest in the refrigerator for at least 2 hours.
10. Now turn the oven on to 250°C.
11. Once the hours passed, take the casserole and put it in oven for at least 1 hour.
12. To check if it is ready after 60 minutes, try to insert a knife to the inside. If this goes out clean, it will mean that the whole liquid has grown thick and that the casserole is ready to be serve.
13. It can be preserve in the refrigerator for maximum 3-4 days.

Here's Mom Wheeler's casserole, a simple recipe that will decidedly make the house warmer and the guests satisfied. Enjoy your meal!

Crispy mini-meatballs

The mini-meatballs are a dish that in America is often cooked, its facility and the delicious taste that it adapts him to every palate. We have thought to an unusual addition to this recipe: the crispy. Yes, exactly what Dustin gives to eat to the small Dart before discovering that in reality it is a Demogorgon. The small monster loves the crispy, and certainly Dustin too. We're going to prepare for them the Crispy mini-meatballs.

Ingredients (x4 people):
- 100 mls of ketchup
- 2 spoons of cane sugar
- 450 gs of ground beef
- 250 gs of ground pork
- 100 mls of pancakes dough (in America it is known as Bisquik)
- 1 pinch of salt
- 1 pinch of pepper
- 1 onion
- 1 egg
- 1 crispy candybar

Preparation:
1. Make to pre-heat the oven to 230°C.

2. Now take a bowl and poured 70 mls of ketchup and cane sugar in. Mix for well with a ladle and then let it rest.
3. Take another container and introduce the ground beef, the pork's one, the Bisquik, the onion, the egg, the pepper and the salt.
4. Work the mixture with the hands up to make to amalgamate well the ingredients.
5. Now pour the mixture in the bowl with ketchup and cane sugar, and then mix again.
6. Once the mixture will be homogeneous, put it on a great paper-baking sheet and thin it with a rolling pin.
7. Now take a knife and divide it in 12 breads.
8. Take the baking-pan to stencils and introduce the mixture to the inside.
9. With a brush, take the remained ketchup and brush it in the surfaces of the meatballs.
10. Bake it for 20-30 minutes, until the meat inside does reach 50°C.
11. When the meatballs will be ready, you extract the baking-pan from the oven and let it all to rest a few minutes.
12. In the meantime, crumble with the hands the crispy candy-bar on the table, just as Dustin makes to feed Dart.
13. Now take the crumbs and spread them overall the meatballs abundantly.

The crispy mini-meatballs are a delicious and easy dish to prepare, that unites sweet and salty in an only amazing taste. The boys of Stranger Things would certainly appreciate it. Enjoy your meal!

Meatloaf, green bean and mashed potatoes

Karen Wheeler, Mike's mother, is certainly the cook that engage more to prepare great dinner for the family. According to what her children say, she is also very good. In the second episode of the first season, when all the boys were invited to dinner at Wheeler's, the lady cooked the Meatloaf with green bean and mashed potatoes, a typical recipe in the years '80 for the American families. Let's see how it's made.

Ingredients (x6 people):
- 600 gs of minced thin meat
- 1 teaspoon of salt
- 1 egg
- 1 pinch of nutmeg
- 50 gs of Parmesan cheese
- 80 gs of grated bread
- 350 gs of spinaches
- 100 gs of sliced speck
- 4 eggs
- Green bean
- 200 mls of milk
- 2 envelopes of mashed potatoes

Preparation:
1. Take a bowl and put the meat, the salt, 1 egg, the nutmeg and the parmesan cheese inside.
2. Mix well with the hands. While you are working the dough, pour few to the time also the grated bread.
3. When it becomes a homogeneous mixture, stretch on the table a wide sheet of paper baking and position the composure above.
4. Gently crush it, and then take another sheet of paper baking, then put it above it.
5. Turn on the oven to 200°C.
6. With a rolling pin, the dough, until it becomes thin and rectangular.
7. Now take the spinaches and scatter them for the whole surface, then do the same with the slices of speck.
8. Now grab the eggs and position them to the beginning of one of the greatest sides of the mixture.
9. Now helping you with the paper baking that there is under, roll up the meatloaf with attention, finally closing it to candy with the paper.
10. Now take a baking-pan, put the meatloaf inside and then introduce it in oven.
11. Let it cook for 45 minutes.
12. In the meantime, take a frying pan and jump the green bean with a thread of oil.
13. Take a pot and pour the milk in.
14. Once it's boiling, turn the burner off, then pour the mashing potatoes envelope in, then salty. Mix with a wood ladle, until it will create a dense and homogeneous form.

15. Time of cooking spent, take the meatloaf out, then remove the paper oven and cut it to slices.
16. Put the meatloaf slices in the dishes with contour of green bean and mashed potatoes.

Mrs Wheeler's meatloaf is ready. Taste it in family!

Upsidedown Turkey with Coke

Correctly cooking a turkey is not an easy enterprise. You need to protect the meat inside and to watch out that dry land doesn't remain too much. Mike's mother is a very good cook and knows well as to cook the turkey. We want to dedicate to her this revisited recipe, so that she could propose it to her children for the Thanksgiving Day. Here to you, the Upsidedown Turkey with Coke.

Ingredients: (x 12 people)
- 350 gs of egg noodles
- 300 gs of thin beef
- 6 onions
- 1 clove of garlic
- 200 mls of tomato sauce
- 200 gs of vegetable cheese
- 230 gs of sour cream
- 200 gs of cheese Cheddar
- Rosemary
- 1 bottle 1,5 liter Coke

Preparation:
1. First, you have to remove the turkey from the freezer and calculate the time according to the weight. It will need about 5 hours for every kilo. If it wasn't in the freezer and you have just bought it, ignore the point 1.

2. Take therefore the turkey, put a pair of clean gloves, and, insert the hand to its interior, then remove all the organs and the chitterlings.
3. Now position it inside a great baking-pan.
4. Turn a big pot on and put the garlic and the cut onions inside. When they are browned for well, add the beef, the tomato sauce, the rosemary and let it cook.
5. When the cooking will have reached the correct point, put the turkey belly-up and fill it with the mixture. Let it then rest to room temperature for at least 2 hours.
6. Now turn the oven on to 200°C, and when it is warm, insert the turkey inside for 30 minutes. When half an hour is passed, lower the temperature to 160°C and let it cook for 2 hours.
7. While the turkey roasts, pick up a pot and pour the Coke with Cheedar and sour cream, then let it cook with slow fire.
8. After the two hours, take the turkey out and check the temperature of the thighs and the skin with a kitchen thermometer. The first one must precisely be to 50°C and the second to 40°C. If the temperature is not right, let the turkey cook again.
9. Throw it out then, and take a kitchen brush. Start to spread the Coke with cheese and cream for the whole perimeter of the animal. In the end, let it rest at room temperature for 20-25 minutes before cutting it.

The Upsidedown Turkey with Coke is ready!

French Onion Barb

Barbara Holland is surely one of the characters who Stranger Things fans miss more. Nancy's big and faithful friend, she didn't deserve the end she has made. This dish is a sort of soup with inside the head of the girl, perhaps a bit grisly but surely perfect for the evening of Halloween. This dish will give a march in more to the party and it will surprise your guests.

Ingredients (x4 people):
- 450 gs flour
- 10 gs yeast
- 1 glass of water
- 1 onion
- 2 eggs
- Chicken soup
- 4 slices of Emmenthal
- Butter
- Salt
- Pepper

Preparation:
1. The first step you have to do is to prepare the dough you need for modelling Barb's face. Take a bowl and prepare the mix with 450 flour gs, 10 gs of yeast and a glass of water. Once ready pick it up and lean it on a plan, it will be your base of departure.

2. In the meantime, start to cut the onion and divide it in two parts. Cut it of long so that to get some filaments. Put a little pot on the fire and prepare the chicken soup with whole pieces to give flavor.
3. To this point, stretch the dough creating an oval (you must use it for the face) form, remembering to pool out less than half of it, so that to define subsequently eyes, eyebrows, nose and hair.
4. With calm, create little balls of dough and use it to do the eyes, then form eyebrows and nose. With some longer and thinner pieces, you can make the hair. To attach better them, beats two eggs in a bowl and with a brush pass them on the zone of your interest as if they were attached.
5. Now put the onion in a non-stick pot to brown with a spins of oil and, once done, add 2-3 pieces of butter, then cook it all with low flame to form a cream. Add the warm chicken soup and let it cook in a frying pan for about 10-15 minutes. Now turn it off.
6. You are ready to pour the dough inside a round container. Pour in the sides the soup and the onions. Slightly also mix and chop above the pieces of emmenthal, trying to reach the edge of the heat-resistant pan or container.
7. To this point, bake it to 180° for about 10 minutes.

At the end of the cooking, you French Onion Barb will be ready. Appalling as ever.

Divine French Fries

The first time we met Eleven, we have roused her to steal french fries inside a diner. The way she devoured it, makes us feel sorry for her and her hunger. We want then to propose, in honor of that first episode of Stranger Things, some innovative fries, that the girl would certainly love. We're going to prepare the Divine French Fries.

Ingredients (x4 people):
- 3-4 potatoes
- white truffle oil
- parsley
- salt
- Pepper

Preparation:
1. Turn the oven on and make it heat. The correct temperature is to 180°C.
2. Start shaving the potatoes and cut them, not too much small and not too much thick.
3. After that, take a baking-pan and uniformly distribute the potatoes. Avoid putting otherwise one above the other because the cooking won't be correct.
4. Add the pepper and the salt. You will also add it after the cooking therefore don't exaggerate.

5. Bake the potatoes remembering to check and turn them every now and then. In this way, they won't stick to the baking-pan. If you want, you can add a thread of oil to give them a gilding and an extra level crisp.
6. Let them cook for about 25-30 minutes.
7. Once ready, make them cool for a few minutes.
8. Put the chips in a bowl and then add the truffle oil, it will give them a very particular and savory taste.
9. Finally add the parsley and other salt.

A recipe that will make you try the chips in different way, from the unique taste. Once they'll be ready, pay attention, Eleven could wander around... After all these are the Divine French fries! Taste them in company!

Scrambled Eggs

Scrambled Eggs are a lot more than a dish; they represent a monument of the Anglo-Saxon culture: in USA or in the United Kingdom, they will usually be there during breakfast. They are actually one of the true elements that unite the two countries together. However, it is certain they also find some point in common watching Stranger Things, and they cannot wait to try all the recipes named in the series. If you want to try too to prepare the Scrambled Eggs, here is a simple recipe to taste them to the best.

Ingredients (for 2 people):
- 4 eggs
- 4 of milk
- 1 stick of butter
- Salt
- Pepper

Preparation:
1. Take the eggs, and break them in a deep dish. You remember that four is the necessary number of eggs for a preparation for two people: if the scrambled eggs will be only for you, you can reduce the number to 2, if they are for the whole family you have to multiply them.
2. Add salt and pepper to the eggs, and beat it all with a fork. The key of the scrambled eggs is really how you use the fork,

which helps to maintain not only the taste, but also the naturalness of the recipe.
3. After that, take a frying non-stick pan and make to heat some butter inside it.
4. Now add the beaten eggs, and start to mix with a wooden spoon: turn and keep on turning, so to get a usual and compact mixture as if the eggs had been, for the note, scrambled.
5. Let cook the eggs for about 4 minutes with low burner. Watch out the consistence: the mixture must solidify, but the eggs must remain always soft.

So voilà, your scrambled eggs are ready. Easy, true? If you want a real Anglo-Saxon breakfast, you can serve her close to bacon and toast, but they are very well also alone, kind for the ones as Italians accustoms to a lighter breakfast. You can also taste them on the waffle as Eleven would do. Enjoy your meal!

Spinaches with two cheeses sandwich

To create some proper recipes for the theme Stranger Things we're going to play around as we like it, always keeping in mind some tastes, some colours and the preferences the protagonists prefer. We are sure that Eleven and the other ones would love these sandwiches to the green colour of mud, which remembers the turbid air of the Upsidedown. We're going to prepare the delicious Spinaches with two cheeses sandwich.

Ingredients: (x 8 sandwiches)
- 115g of butter
- 200g of cheese (caciotta or provolone)
- 200g of cheese Cheddar
- 18g of salt
- 15g of avocado
- 40g of spinaches
- 16 slices of Wonder Bread

Preparation:
1. Start taking a pot and put the butter, the cheeses, the salt and the avocado inside. Mix it all with calm and for well, until the mixture it amalgamate and all the clumps disappear.
2. Now add the spinaches and keep on turning with attention.

3. Take the iron to toast the bread. If you don't have it, a big frying pan will be all right.
4. Now prepare eight slices of bread on the table and, when the mixture is ready and well warm, start to fill every slice.
5. When you will have stuffed all the bread, take the other slices and put them above to close the sandwiches.
6. Now position a sandwich behind the other, according to how much they are, to cook in the iron, in the electric oven or in the frying pan.
7. Make to toast the bread 3 minutes for every side, if it is in frying pan. If you use the oven there will be no need to turn them, 3 minutes in total will be all right.
8. When they'll be ready, remove the sandwiches and prepare them in the dishes.
9. Leave them to cool for two minutes now, then cut them to half and serve.

Here are the Spinaches with two cheeses sandwiches. They must be served well as snack to your children or as a lunch for the whole family. They are healthy, good and definitely savory. Enjoy your meal!

WAFFLE SALATI

Mini waffles cheeseburger

When we met Eleven, after having been surprised by the caterer to steal the french fries, he offered her a savory cheeseburger, that she has literally devoured. Everything happened before Mike made her try the waffles, and since then any food had no competition. We thought then about creating some cheeseburgers that the girl could like, because instead of bread, we will put waffles there! Here to you the mini waffles cheeseburger.

Ingredients: (x2 people)
- 150g of flour 0
- 2 teaspoons of yeast powdered
- 1 teaspoon of sugar
- 2 eggs
- 50g of butter
- 100 mls of milk
- 3 pinches of salt
- 100 gs of beef
- 3 slices of cheese Cheddar
- Mayonnaise
- Ketchup
- Maple syrup
- 1 little tomato
- 1 leaf of lettuce
- 1 onion

Preparation:
1. Prepare the things for the dough of the waffles. Take therefore two pots of average greatness and the eggs.
2. Beat the eggs and divide in a container the egg whites and in the other the yolks.
3. Start to mount the egg whites, and add the sugar to the yolks. Work well these last until you will eliminate all the clumps.
4. Now heat a small pot and make the butter lining inside, after that let it rest.
5. Pour the egg whites and the butter in the bowl with the yolks, and keep always on mixing.
6. Now add to the dough one by one, the flour, the milk, the yeast and 1 pinch of salt.
7. Make to correctly amalgamate the mixture and let it rest.
8. In the meantime, take another frying pan and make it heat. With the beef create some small meatballs. After that, make them cook for a few minutes for every side and then add two pinches of salt.
9. Now grab a new bowl and mix the mayonnaise, the ketchup and the syrup of maple.
10. Heat the waffle iron and poured a half ladle in, to create the miniskirts waffles.
11. When they will be ready, put them one by one above the table and start to position a meatball for slice. Put then above cheese's slices, the tomato, the lettuce and the onion.
12. Finally sprinkle the all with sauces and syrup' mix and then cover the sandwiches with the other waffle.

Enjoy your meal!!

Eleven's Eggo Sandwiches

Thanks to the passion of Eleven, the stramble girl of the show, for the Eggo Waffles, as appalling recipes can be invented you inspire to the show of the moment: Stranger Things. If you also have become some series dependent, you have to try all the strangest recipes connected to the show. Here to you the Eleven's Eggo Sandwiches.

Ingredients (x4 people):
- 150g of flour 0
- 2 teaspoons of yeast powdered
- 1 teaspoon of sugar
- 5 eggs
- 50g of butter
- 100 mls of milk
- ground meat
- 1 pinch of salt
- 1 pinch of pepper
- parsley
- garlic
- white wine

Preparation:
1. Start preparing the dough for the mini waffle. Take 2 eggs and separate the egg whites from the yolks. Position a pot on the

burner and make the butter melt. In another container, make the egg whites mount.
2. In a pot, mix the egg whites with the sugar until all the clumps will disappear. Pour the cool melted butter inside. Turn it all with a lot of patience and later, add the egg whites.
3. When it became a dense and homogeneous mixture, you can insert the flour, the salt, the milk and the yeast. Let it rest.
4. In the meantime, prepare the meatballs of ground meat. In a pot, start cooking the ground meat with the garlic, the parsley, the salt, the pepper and the white wine. Leave everything to cook for about 20 minutes until the meat won't be ready.
5. Now take the three remained eggs and pour them into a pot, after 1 minute maltreat them with a fork.
6. Pour the content with the meat in another container and form the meatballs.
7. Make to heat the waffle iron and pour a small ladle in to create some miniskirts waffles.
8. When every mixture will have reached the right cook, take the mini waffles and prepare them on the table, add first the scrambled eggs and above the meatballs, then close them with another mini waffle in surface.

The Eleven's Eggo Sandwich will be ready to be tasted, possibly warm.

Bacon and chicken waffle sandwiches

Chicken and waffles. It do not seem an ideal combination, but for a Stranger Things' dependent, by now we know that, as Jonathan says, what's normal never does the difference in the world. We have wanted therefore to create this strange mix, which will be more savory than ever. And if we even add the bacon? Let's see together what come out from here.

Ingredients (x4 people):
- 100 gs flour
- 30 gs of sugar
- 5 gs of baking soda
- 10 gs of yeast powdered
- 1 pinch of salt
- 1 pinch of pepper
- 2 eggs
- 15 gs of melted butter
- 245 mls of buttermilk
- 3 slices of bacon
- 100 gs of cheese Cheddar
- 2 shallots (green onions) cut to thin slices

Fried chicken:
- 2 big wings of chicken cut to half

- 150 mls of buttermilk
- 100 gs of maize starch
- 50 gs flour
- 1 pinch of salt
- 1 pinch of Cayenna chilli
- 1 pinch of garlic powder
- 1 pinch of black pepper
- 1 pinch of paprika
- Oil for frying

Preparation:
Waffles:
1. Preheat the waffle iron.
2. Take a big bowl, and put together flour, sugar, bicarbonate, yeast, salt and pepper.
3. Mix it all gently.
4. Break the eggs in a bowl apart and start to beat them.
5. Add melted butter and buttermilk. By helping you with a wood spoon, mix the all to amalgamate it.
6. Add the bacon, the cheese Cheddar and the shallots.
7. Anoint the plate for waffles.
8. Pour a ladle of mixture in the iron; therefore, let it cook until you get the desired gilding: should not want us more than 4 minutes.

Fried chicken and buttermilk
1. Pour in frying pan the oil to fry.
2. Put the wings of chicken in a big bowl, therefore cover them with buttermilk and, if you want, barbecue sauce.

3. Mix it all together until the buttermilk will completely cover the chicken.
4. Cover the chicken with plastic wrap, and then put in the refrigerator: let it cool for at least 30 minutes.
5. Take a flat dish, and unite maize starch, flour, salt, Cayenna chilli, garlic powder, paprika and black pepper.
6. Take the wings of chicken, and dip them in the mixture with maize starch and flour, then leave them to rest for at least 10 minutes.
7. Put the wings of chicken, one by one, in the frying pan with the oil, therefore fry for 7 minutes doing well attention to turn them more times.

The sandwich
1. Put a slice of cheese cheddar on every wing of chicken, and let it melt in the oven.
2. Put the wings of chicken on a quarter of waffle.
3. Add tomatoes or lettuce or anything wants.

A particular, strange and savory recipe!

Green slime waffle sandwich

When we find us in front to a dish like this, obviously Stranger Things will come to our minds. The Upsidedown is a different dimension with a rotten atmosphere and appalling beings. We have thought therefore to create a delicious dish, that Eleven would love because of the waffle, but approaching it to the Upsidedown world, from which the girl will always try to run away. Here to you the Green Slime Waffle Sandwich.

Ingredients (x4 people)::
- 150g of flour 0
- 2 teaspoons of yeast powdered
- 1 teaspoon of sugar
- 2 eggs
- 70g of butter
- 100 mls of milk
- Gouda Pesto
- 100 gs of boiled ham
- slices of cheese Emmenthal

Preparation:
1. First, prepare the waffle composure; you will need two of them to do a sandwich. Take then two different bowls, in one you put the yolks of the eggs and in the other the egg whites.

2. Now begin to mount the egg whites. In the meantime, you can also add in the container of the yolks the sugar and mix it all for well with a spoon, until all the clumps will disappear.
3. Now position a small pot on the burner and make 50 gs of butter to melt, and later let it cool.
4. After it have reached temperature, pour the butter in the container with the yolks and then the egg whites. Do everything with calm so that the ingredients perfectly gets married among them while mixing.
5. When you will got a beautiful homogeneous mixture, you will be ready to add the salt, the milk, the flour and the yeast. Pour them inside one by one, always with the due caution, the let it rest.
6. In the meantime, turn the grill on. When it's well warm, position the cheese above, with slow fire.
7. Turn the waffle iron on, and start to pour us an half of the composure inside.
8. When the first waffle will be ready, raise it from the iron and pour the remaining dough inside. In the while, start to compose the sandwich, positioning the grilled cheese before, then the boiled ham, and finally an abundant quantity of Gouda pesto.
9. As soon as also the second waffle will be ready, pick it up and put it to cover the sandwich.

Your Green Slime Waffle Sandwich is ready to be serve in dreadful way!

Bacon, onion and mozzarella waffle sandwich

Waffles are not only delicious, they are by now an aspect of the breakfast of which the Americans cannot do without, just as Eleven. But their best advantage is that they are extremely versatile and they are good with everything. They can be eaten both sweets or salty and the result is guaranteed. Here to you a new recipe that the protagonist of Stranger Things would love, the Bacon, onion and mozzarella waffle sandwich.

Ingredients (x2 people):
- 100g of flour 0
- 1 teaspoons of yeast powdered
- 1/2 teaspoon of sugar
- 4 eggs
- 30 gs of butter
- 100 mls of milk
- 1 pinch of salt
- vegetable of season (spinaches, rucola, cabbage)
- 1 mozzarella
- 1 onion
- 1 pinch of black pepper
- mustard

Preparation:

1. You will need two waffles to create the sandwich, therefore begun by their dough. Take two different bowls and two eggs, in one you will put the egg whites and in the other the yolks.
2. Mount the egg whites and in the yolks add there instead the sugar. Turn the mixture until the clumps will disappear.
3. In a pot, after you make it heat, pour the butter and make it melt. Now leave it to cool.
4. Now pour the butter and the egg whites in the container of the yolks and work well it with calm.
5. When the mixture will be homogeneous, add one ingredient at a time, departing from the flour, then the salt, the milk and the yeast. Mix the all for well and then let it rest.
6. Take two frying pans and position them in two different burners. After having put a thread of oil in both, in the first one make the vegetables of season cook, and in the other put the bacon to crisp.
7. In the meantime, cut the mozzarella and the onion.
8. Make to heat the waffle iron, and as soon as it will be ready, pour a half composure in. When the first waffle will have taken form, get it away and pour the remaining mix.
9. Position the first waffle on a dish as the base of the sandwich, and as first layer put the crisp bacon there.
10. After that, make a sprinkle of mustard and go by the lower part toward the other with the following ingredients: mozzarella, vegetables, onions, pepper, still mustard.
11. To this point, the second waffle will be ready, and you have to put it as cover of the sandwich.

Enjoy your meal!!

Eggo Waffle

We all know by now Eleven's obsession for Eggo Waffles, she would set them as main meal every hour of the day. Thanks to eggs' great deal, they represent the necessary source of proteins to defeat the bad Demogorgone. True Eggo Waffles are born in 1953, 'til they has been acquired by the industrial chain Kellogg's in the '70s. We're going to prepare the recipe of these delicious Waffles with the addition of some original and terryfing ingredients, in perfect theme Stranger Things.

Ingredients (x 10 people)
- 250g of flour 0
- 4 teaspoons of baking powder
- 2 eggs
- 75g of butter
- 375 mls of warm milk
- 1 stem celery
- 1 onion
- 1 clove garlic
- 1 pinch of salt
- 400 mls chicken soup
- 10g thyme
- 5g sage
- 2 leaves parsley

Preparation:
1. Start taking the eggs and separating the egg whites and the yolks. Now make the egg whites mount, and in another pot you let melt the butter.
2. Now take another bowl and pour the yolks in with sugar, then mix it together until it is a no clumps mixture. Add the melted butter and mix it all gently. Pour also mounted egg whites in and then keep on working the doug.
3. Now add to the mixture, flour, salt, milk and yeast and knead it well. Leave everything to rest.
4. In the meantime, start to cut in little pieces the celery, the onion and the garlic. Once you're done, add the three ingredients in the mixture and let it cook for about 8 minutes.
5. Now pour inside the pot the chicken soup, the thyme, the sage and the salt. You have to keep on working until it boils. Now turn the burner off and add parsley in the mixture. Lei it rest.
6. Now take the waffle iron and make it heat. Once it reaches the right temperature, pour the mixture inside one ladle at a time. Once ready, move them gently to the dishes and serve.

Here ready the Waffle Eggos adapted Stranger Things' style. Will you dare taste them and help the boys to fight Demogorgon?

Fried chicken, grilled cheese and pickled cherries sandwich

There are meals that taken alone, they could seem vulgar, almost rough. With the addition of few ingredients however, all can change, and they becomes some refined and savory dishes. The very beloved waffles of Eleven can be therefore turned into something appetizing, and still result good in appalling way. We're going to prepare fried chicken, grilled cheese and pickled cherries sandwich.

Ingredients:
- 150g of flour 0
- 2 teaspoons of yeast powdered
- 1 teaspoon of sugar
- 2 eggs
- 70g of butter
- 100 mls of milk
- smoked cheese
- some piece of okra
- 1 breast of boned chicken
- pickled cherries
- 1 pinch of salt

Preparation:
1. For first thing, take a frying pan and a grate. In the first one, put the breast of chicken to make it fry. In the other one,

position nearby the gumbo from a part and the cheese in the other to make them grill both.

2. In the meantime, prepare the dough for the waffles. Take then the eggs and separate the yolks from the egg whites with attention, in two different bowls. In the while, you can make the butter melt in a small pot.

3. Now mount the egg whites and in the other bowl mix the yolks with the sugar, turning with delicacy until all the clots will disappear.

4. Add to the yolks the egg whites that you have mounted and then pour the butter in.

5. Now that the dough has become enough dense, add the salt, the flour, the milk and the yeast, and emphatically mix. Left it all a few minutes to rest.

6. The cheese by now would have been ready; therefore, you can withdraw it from the grate. Leave still instead the gumbo, which requires more time. Remove the chicken from the frying pan.

7. Make now the waffle iron to heat, or in alternative that for the pancakes that it is more spacious.

8. Take the mixture of waffles and pour it with caution inside the iron, until a mixture it becomes uniform.

9. When the big waffle will be ready, get away from the iron and position it in a container to season it.

10. Put therefore the cheese on the base, then above it put the fried chicken, spreading well pieces everywhere.

11. To his point, it only remains the cherries, so position them on the surface. Now take an extremity of the waffle and turn upside-down it as to close a sandwich.

12. Turn again the iron on and position the waffle, until becomes crispy.
13. Now extract the waffle from the iron and serve warm.

Here ready the fried chicken, grilled cheese and pickled cherry sandwich. Enjoy your meal!

Bacon and Cheddar Waffle

Have you ever tried the salted Waffle? The variation rich of proteins with bacon and Cheddar will be an attractive discovery, rapid and creative, to taste with your friends. Very loved by the "stramble girl" and from her four small friends, you will find out a new way to eat the waffles while you are enjoying an episode of Stranger Things.

Ingredients:
- 500 grs of potatoes
- 150 grs whipped cream
- 130 grs of Cheddar
- 2 eggs
- 70 grs flour
- 30 grs d butter
- 120 grs of bacon
- salt
- pepper

Preparation:
1. Take a bowl and pour in the eggs, the whipped cream, the pepper and the salt. Slowly also add the flour and mix it all with energy.
2. Shave now the potatoes and cut them to bits. Once done, throw them in a mixer. After that, add the potatoes to the yet

prepared mixture and mix in such way to create an only amalgam.

3. Remember that instead of beating the potatoes, it is also possible to simply grate them and to add them in the mixture, until they become part of the mixture.
4. Take now a little pot and heat the butter until it will melt. Then add it to the mixture together, with Cheddar and the cut bacon. You finally mix everything. Dough is ready.
5. Now take a waffle iron (the ideal would be well warm) and anoint it with oil, so that to avoid the stick of the mixture.
6. The mixture must be cooked for different minutes (3 will be enough) until when the waffle will have a gilded colour. Once they're crushed, don't wait until they're cool, immediately add above other cheddar and bacon. Cheese will become melt and bacon warm.

A different waffle from the usual one. It can be consumed both to lunch and to dinner or sprouts. Try them with your strange friends!

Grilled cheese and fried chicken waffle

An eccentric and innovative recipe, just as the characters and the stories of Stranger Things. All the fans of the series at least once have desired to try to compose thousand recipes with the waffles Eleven loves so much. Why not do those salty? We're going to prepare the Grilled cheese and fried chicken waffle.

Ingredients:
- 100 gs flour 0
- 1 teaspoon of yeast powder
- ½ sugar's teaspoon
- 1 egg
- 30 gs of butter
- 1 pinch of salt
- 70 mls of milk
- 200 gs of breast of chicken
- 3 slices of cheese Cheddar
- 1 teaspoon of honey
- spicy sauce

Preparation:
1. You will need an only big waffle, therefore initiated to prepare the dough. Slightly take two pots, a small and bigger one.

2. Now divide the egg and, in the first bowl you will pour the egg white, while in the second the yolk.
3. Stiffen the egg white and then add the sugar to the yolk. Work well until the clumps will be entirely disappeared.
4. Now make a pot to heat and let the butter melt inside, after that leave it to cool.
5. Pour therefore the butter inside the bowl with the yolk and later also the egg white. Always keep on working the mixture and, one by one, add flour, salt, sugar, milk and yeast. Mixing for well and later let it rest.
6. Now take a frying pan and fry the breast of chicken. Then in a grill, make the cheese melt.
7. To this point also positioned above a burner the waffle iron and, when it is well warm, pour the whole mixture inside.
8. In the while that the wafer is beginning to form, take a teaspoon and verse gently the honey overall the surface.
9. Remove then the chicken from the frying pan and lean it on the kitchen paper to absorb the oil.
10. Now you have to remove the waffle from the iron and lean it on a dish.
11. Cut the chicken to small slices, and then crumble them on the waffle with care. Add above also the grilled cheese and then pour an abundant quantity of spicy sauce.
12. Serve and enjoy!

Bacon, Sriracha syrup and fried chicken waffles

If it happens to you too, to be awake the whole night to look at the series Stranger Things because you cannot wait to discover what it will happen in the next episode, you have become some show dependent. Don't worry tough, it happens once you've been affectionate to Eleven and to her friends. If you have so much time to pass glued to the screen, we give you a fast recipe to prepare and to taste while you are doing that. Enjoy the Bacon, Sriracha syrup and fried chicken waffles.

Ingredients:
- 150g of flour 0
- 2 teaspoons of yeast powdered
- 1 teaspoon of sugar
- 2 eggs
- 70g of butter
- 100 mls of milk
- 1 pinch of salt
- 1 breast of chicken
- 1 teaspoon of honey
- 30 mls of maple syrup
- 20 mls of Sriracha syrup
- Smoked bacon
- 3 slices of applesauce

Preparation:
1. Start to prepare the dough to create your waffles. Take therefore two bowls and the eggs.
2. In the greatest container put the yolks, and in the other the egg whites.
3. Make to mount the egg whites, and in the meantime, put the sugar in the yolks.
4. Work for well the mixture until all the clumps will disappear.
5. To this point make a pot to heat and melt 50 gs of butter until it becomes liquid.
6. Now pour the butter inside the mixture with the yolks and later even the egg whites.
7. After that, always keeping on mixing, pour in, one to the time the following ingredients: milk, flour, yeast and salt.
8. Work all for well and then let it rest.
9. To this point, take another bowl and pour the maple syrup and Sriracha one in, and mix them together.
10. In the meantime, fry the chicken breast.
11. Now put the waffle iron to heat, and when it is hot, pour an half of the composure.
12. Once ready, raise the first waffle and pour the remaining mixture to realize the second.
13. In the meantime, place the first one on a dish and start to stuff the sandwich.
14. First, pour an half of the mixture of syrups, after the breast of chicken, then the smoked bacon and finally the remaining syrup.
15. After that take the second waffle and close the sandwich.
16. In surface, pour the melted butter that has remain and then the honey.

Enjoy your meal!!

Pizza Waffle

Stranger Things lovers know well that Eleven find the waffles delicious, something you cannot do without. With these special waffles, it is possible to make thousand different recipes to taste to breakfast, lunch or dinner. To satisfy the strange girl and to combine the waffles with a unique meal, we have decided to create the Pizza Waffle. It could seem an insane or not pleasant to the palate thing, but keep on reading and you will change your mind. We're going to prepare the Pizza Waffle.

Ingredients(x2 people):
- 150g of flour 0
- 2 teaspoons of yeast powdered
- 2 eggs
- 50g of butter
- 1 teaspoon of sugar
- 100 mls of milk
- 2 spoons of tomato sauce
- 1 mozzarella
- 2 leaves of basil

Preparation:
1. Prepare first the waffle dough, which later you will need as base of our super pizza. Separate then the eggs in two different

bowls between egg whites and yolks. In the meantime, melt the butter inside a pot and let it cool.

2. Mount the egg whites and then mix the yolks with the sugar to get a dense and homogeneous mixture. To this point, also pour the cool butter in. Keep on slowly working the mixture with a lot of delicacy. Once that you will have ended, add the egg whites.
3. Keep on always mixing and then add flour, salt, yeast and milk. Never stop turning with the ladle.
4. Turn the oven on, and in the while, heat the waffle iron. If you don't have it, in alternative you can use the pancakes one.
5. When the iron will be hot, pour the waffle dough inside, not one ladle at a time, but all together, or however enough to cover the frying pan so that to make the base for a pizza.
6. Once you create the giant waffle, you can raise it from the iron. Now put it on the table. Pour above the tomato exactly as you do for the pizza leaving the open moulding.
7. Put the Pizza Waffle two minutes in oven, in that way you will toast the base, and in the meantime, cut the mozzarella to small dices.
8. Extract the pizza from the oven and scatter above it the mozzarella. Put again in oven and let it cook for 10-15 minutes.
9. To this point, pull the all out and lean on the centre two basil leaves.

Your Pizza Waffle is ready to be serve and taste!

DOLCE

Ginger syrup

The ginger syrup is known for its nutritional and curative benefits. It's good for the throat, it favours the digestion, it improves the arthritis and the blood circulation. Well, the protagonists of Stranger Things know that, and they use this syrup to garnish many of their recipes. It's perfect on the waffles so loved by Eleven. We're going to prepare the homemade ginger syrup.

Ingredients:
- 250 gs of white sugar
- 250 mls of water
- 50 gs of fresh ginger

Preparation:
1. Start to shave the ginger, cut it in small pieces and hold it in a saucer or container.
2. Now take a pot, and pour the sugar in. Turn the flame on with low fire.
3. Immediately start to add the water and, in the while, keep on mixing.
4. When you will end with the water, put the pieces of ginger inside. Keep on mixing.
5. After only a few minutes, the mixture will become dense and homogeneous. Try not to form clumps. Now you can turn the burner off.

6. To this point, let it rest a few other minutes and then directly filter the mixture in the bottle that you will use for the syrup, better if it's made of glass. The pieces of ginger must also be removed, as all the solid composure in the syrup.
7. Let it all to cool. Once done, the syrup will be usable to garnish desserts or other preparations of confectioneries.
8. You can preserve it in the refrigerator.

Your ginger syrup is ready; you can finally taste its delicious drink and use it to draw all its benefits, just as the protagonists of Stranger Things do!

Pickled Cherries

We have figured out by now that every episode of Stranger Things contains numerous dishes and recipes that the characters taste every day. But if we tried to reproduce a recipe that has never been described in the series, but our beniamins could still like? And what is better than a recipe in perfect horror style as a beautiful pot of pickled cherries, with a color that remembers so much of the human blood? Today we're going to prepare Pickled Cherries, but you better watch out, Demogorgon loves blood, you know.

Ingredients:
- 2 kilos mature cherries
- 700 ml red wine vinegar
- 350 grams of sugar
- 40 grams of salt
- 1 orange peel
- 1 pinch of black pepper
- 2 cinnamon sticks
- 1 spoon of coriander seeds
- 1 laurel leaf

Preparation
1. First of all, you need to take the cherries and, with a toothpick, start poking them for the whole round surface.

2. Then bring a jar of glass with a closable cover and, one by one, you have to introduce the cherries inside.
3. Put a pot on the stove now, and pour in vinegar, salt, grated orange peel, black pepper, laurel leaf, cinnamon sticks, coriander seeds and let it cook.
4. Every now and then you have to stir to make the ingredients fold together.
5. Once you'll notice the first little bubbles, and so vinegar is reaching the boiling point, you need to reduce the burner to a minimum, and then let it cook for other 10 minutes.
6. Take off the pot at this point and leave everything to get cold for other 10 minutes. If it won't be enough, also 20.
7. You now bring the jar containing cherries and start to pour the liquid in with a ladle. Go on until you have completely cover them to the surface.
8. If the liquid has not become cold yet, leave the jar still open. Then close it well with the cover and seal it.

Here you go, the pickled cherries with human blood color are ready, in perfect terryfing style Stranger Things. Remember that to give the flavor liquid to the cherries you must leave them at least a few days in the refrigerator before tasting them. Then they can be stored in the refrigerator for maximum 1 month.

Nutella Cream

What about Nutella? National Italian patrimony, beloved all over the world, even if she also suffers always its fair share of criticisms. In every case, however, Nutella is perfect to garnish desserts, and above all, small gang of Stranger Things finds it delicious. Here then a brief recipe for Nutella Cream, useful for any type of chocolate dessert to offer to the kids.

Ingredients:
- 500 mls milk
- 4 yolks
- 50 gs flour
- 100 gs sugar
- 300 gs Nutella
- 1 vanilla bean (if you don't have it, 1 vanillina packet is all right)

Preparation
1. Heat the milk in a little pot with a vanilla bean.
2. When milk just starts to boil, you can turn the burner off. Immediately you have to remove the little pot from the burner, to prevent the residual heat makes to boil the milk more than necessary.

3. Take a bowl, and start mounting the yolks with the sugar: the mixture that comes out from there must be foamy, then you can it's ready.
4. Now add the flour to yolks and sugar: to do that, you need to use a sieve.
5. Then gradually add warm milk and amalgamate it all to get a dense mixture.
6. Let it simmer for a few minutes.
7. Now put the cream into a bowl, and cover it with plastic wrap: watch out how you do this passage to prevent crusts formation.
8. Now let it all refresh.
9. Now gradually add Nutella to the cream, and mix from the top down to create an uniform mixture.
10. Now leave the cream in the refrigerator to make it cool.

Here you now have your Nutella cream, witch you can spread on delicious Waffles Eleven loves. Or maybe on tarts and, why not, on ice cream. You also can applie it to cakes, especially if dedicated to children. You can prepare for example penguin cake or yogurt cake. However, pay attention not to leave the cream in the refrigerator for more than 3 days: if you want you can freeze it in mono-doses.

Christmas Cupcakes

Stranger Things' first season develops it in a pre-Christmas climate, and because of it Joyce try desperate to reach her child through the lights. In the last episode they celebrate Christmas, but above the happiness knowing Will back home, alive. In honor of this we're going to prepare today the Christmas Cupcakes, perfect and fast for festivities.

Ingredients:
- 120 gs of butter
- 120 gs flour 00
- 120 gs of sugar
- 3 eggs
- 1 tsp of vanilla extract
- 50 gs of chocolate powder
- 2 gs yeast
- 1 pinch of salt
- ½ glass of water
- whipped cream
- vegetable oil
- chocolate frosting
- M&M's

Preparation:

1. Take a bowl and pour in to butter, sugar, chocolate and the vanilla extract. Start to beat the mixture with a whilp and make it mount.
2. Now break the eggs and gently pour them inside, always keeping on working. As soon the mixture will be dense and homogeneous, you place the whip and put a strainer above the bowl.
3. You now sieve the flour and the yeast in and restart to mix gently with a spatula.
4. Now begin to heat the oven to 180°.
5. Take cupcakes wrappers and fill each one of them with the mixture. Bake the cupcakes for 25 minutes.
6. When they'll be ready, take them out and let them refresh. Now you can start garnish them.
7. Above each of them, you put whipped cream, composing a sort of Christmas tree form.
8. After that, you put the black frosting in a sac à poche and then draw some lines around the cream to symbolize lights' string.
9. Now you can finally take the M&M's and spread them above, not too near and not too much for each cupcake. They must seem some light bulbs.

You do the same job with each and you will get some Christmas desserts, in perfect style Stranger Things.

Upsidedown Muffins

Muffins are of the English typical desserts that have been expanded by now in the houses of everybody all over the world, also in Italy. They are easy to be prepare and so good to be tasted. We have decided to suit them for Stranger Things and the living room full of lights of Christmas and letters of Joyce Byers when she talked with her little Will. We're going to prepare the Upsidedown muffins today. We will complete the letters of the English alphabet; therefore, the muffins must be 26.

Ingredients (x4/5 people) :
- 600 gs flour
- 300 gs of sugar
- 110 gs of cocoa
- 270 gs of butter
- 5 eggs
- 300 mls of milk
- 20 gs of yeast
- 220 gs of drops of melting chocolate
- whipped cream
- black frosting
- M&M's

Preparation:
1. Take a bowl and poured inside flour, sugar, cocoa and yeast.
2. Mix the all for well to make it become a homogeneous mixture.
3. Grab a second container and put inside butter (after having it melted and cooled), the eggs and the milk. Amalgamate for well.
4. Turn the oven on to 180°C.
5. After having worked the two mixes, unite them together and then add the drops of chocolate.
6. Mix it all in a way uniform.
7. Now take the stencils for the muffins wrappers, pulling them for 2/3.
8. To this point, insert everything in oven and make them cook for 20 minutes.
9. Now take the muffins out and leave them to cool for 10 minutes.
10. After that, smear with a knife a layer of whipped cream above them all.
11. Let them dry for 5 minutes.
12. Now prepare the muffins in horizontal line one after the other, very near.
13. Introduce the black frosting inside a sac à poche.
14. Write all the letters of the alphabet, one for every muffin with the frosting.
15. Always with the frosting, compose a black line above the letters that it goes from a muffin to the other, as to draw the thread of the Christmas lights.

16. Now prepare an M&M for every muffin, as if they were attached to the thread of the lights and these will be the light bulbs.

You will have created the wall of the living room of Joyce with the Christmas lights and the letters of the alphabet. These muffins are certainly very beautiful to see for the fans of Stranger Things, and delicious for the palate of all the gluttons. Enjoy your meal!

Blood Drops Cake

Cocoa cake is ideal for chocolate's lovers who don't want to venture too much in a binding recipe. If then we add there some small drops of red colour, it becomes a perfect dessert for the fans of Stranger Things. We're going to prepare the Cocoa cake with drops of blood.

Ingredients (x4 people):
- Cocoa Powder (200 gs)
- Milk (170 gs)
- Flour 00 (450 gs)
- Butter (125 gs)
- Sugar (180 gs)
- Eggs (175 gs)
- 30 gs of Nutella
- Red food coloring

Preparation:
1. First melt the butter and leave it warm.
2. Now break the eggs in a bowl, then add the sugar.
3. Climb the mixture on with whips up to get a swollen and foamy consistence.
4. You keep on beating, and in the meantime add the butter, that will be now warm.
5. Now gradually pour the milk, for a mixture uniform.

6. Sieve the cocoa in the bowl, for then to mix the all up to form a well amalgamate mixture.
7. Sieve the flour in the vessel, then you repeat the same procedure of the cocoa: the mixture must always result in a homogeneous amalgam.
8. Butter the chosen mould (in this case, for these quantities of ingredients, the mould will be about 20 cm). The ideal is a springform mould.
9. Pour the mixture inside it.
10. By helping you with a spatula, now level the surface.
11. At this point, we can create the drops. So take a bowl and pour Nutella and food coloring. Mix it enough to make it become a red mixture. If it doesn't become red, add other coloring. Now insert the mixture in a sac à poche.
12. Start cooking the composure in oven preheated to 180 degrees for at least 30 minutes. It is better to put back the cake in the lowest ledge, to make sure that the cooking is ideal. To verify the course of the situation, can make the test of the fences: when it results dry, cocoa cake is ready.
13. You can now compose some drops of red Nutella for the whole surface.

The Cocoa Cake with drops of blood is ready, proper for all the greedy lovers of Stranger Things!

Chocolate Cake

It's all about a dessert very simple to prepare, but rich of goodness, so savory that makes you want to eat it whole! It's super easy to prepare and will be ready in about 30 minutes. You can cook it while you're watching a Stranger Things' episode and the kids would like it a lot. A cake with a unique taste, delightfully savory and soft! We're going to prepare Chocolate Cake.

Ingredients (x2/3 people):
- 200 gs flour
- 100 gs of sugar
- 50 gs of cocoa powder
- yeast powder
- 100 mls of milk
- 1 little envelope of vanilla
- 20 mls of vegetable oil

Cream:
- 50 gs of cane sugar
- Drops of chocolate
- 20 gs of cocoa powder
- 50 mls of warm water

Preparation:
1. Preheat the oven to 180°C so that to reach the right temperature for the cooking of the dessert.

2. In a 2 liters vessel, you have to pour flour, white sugar, cocoa powder and yeast. Then mix it all together.
3. Once the mixture starts to take form and to acquire some body, add milk, oil and vanilla. Mixing it up until it's compact.
4. You put the mixture in an oven mould. Now you are ready for the cooking.
5. Let it cook for 30-35 minutes, until the superior part starts to be stiff. When the cooking is about to finish, you start to prepare the cocoa cream.
6. In a small bowl, mix together cane sugar, cocoa powder and chocolate drops. Now mix gently while you're adding the warm water, so to reach the desired density.
7. Watch out not to add much water and in case you make some mistake, add some other cocoa. Do not let it heat on the burner, that's how this recipe is made. You also have to watch out for the water temperature, better if not so much hot.
8. When the chocolate cake will be ready, turn the oven off and take out the dessert. Now add the cream on the surface and serve warm.
9. In some cases, it is also possible to add some ice cream. Someone also likes to serve the famous chocolate cake with powdered sugar.

A perfect cake for an afternoon with the fans of Stranger Things. A healthy and savory snack, ideal for kids and grown men!

Apple juice cake

The Apple juice cake is a good snack, healthy and savory, which is possible to prepare at home in simple steps. Stranger Things' kids know how to appreciate the good cakes, above all Dustin. It will be a dessert from the unique taste and original. The smell will be even able to inebriate the less mongrels as Lucas. We're going to prepare the Apple juice cake.

Ingredients (x4 people):
- 2 big eggs
- 250 of white sugar
- 20 gs of melted butter
- 300 mls of natural apple juice, not sweetened
- 40 gs flour
- 1 little envelope of yeast
- 30 gs of vanilla extract
- 20 gs cinnamon
- 1 pinch of nutmeg

Preparation:
1. Take a bowl and pour in big eggs and white sugar, then mix them together to get a homogenous composure. Now gently add the melted butter, after you let it cooled. Mix with energy.
2. Add one for time the apple juice and sieved flour. At the end, after having mixed it all, you also add yeast, cinnamon, vanilla and nutmeg. Watch out for cinnamon quantity, inevitable in

the apple juice cake: an excessive dosage could ruin your job and make you realize an inedible dessert!
3. Take a round and tall pot and butter it. Then spread the flour just enough. Now pour the mixture in the pot and bake it to 180°C in pre-heated oven for about 40 minutes.
4. When the dessert will be ready, you can spread powdered sugar all around the surface.
5. It's possible to serve the apple juice cake with whipped cream or with vanilla ice cream, according to tastes.
6. In some varying recipes, somebody make apple juice cake with the cream or the short pastry, but the most famous recipe foresees that is has to be a simple dessert, in which the inevitable taste of the apple must be prevailing.

A dessert that would have the whole company of Stranger Things go crazy! The correct snack for all the children, excellent also for the birthdays.

Upsidedown Vanilla Cake

We know what you're thinking, how can the candid colour of vanilla be associated to the grisly dimension of the Upsidedown? That's exactly how we wanted to play. The real world and the Uspidedown one are two identical dimensions, one the opposite of the other. Therefore, we have thought to mix the sweetness of the vanilla, with some small additions that will not be so nice. We're certain that it will be appreciated! Here is the Upsidedown Vanilla Cake.

Ingredients (x4 people):
- 300 gs flour
- 10 gs of yeast
- 1 pinch of salt
- 170 gs of butter
- Olive oil
- 300 gs of sugar
- 4 eggs
- 15 gs of vanilla extract
- 240 mls of milk
- black frosting
- gummy worms

Frosting
- 230 gs of butter

- 500 gs of powdered sugar
- 1 pinch of salt
- 30 gs of vanilla
- 20 mls of honey
- 100 mls of milk

Preparation:
1. Preheat the oven to 180°C.
2. Take a bowl of averages dimensions and pour in flour, yeast and salt.
3. Add butter, sugar and oil in the mixture; therefore beat it all together for at least 3-4 minutes.
4. Now add 2 eggs once for time, always keeping on mixing.
5. Pour in half of the dry ingredients and you amalgamate it all.
6. Now gradually add milk and vanilla, therefore mix it all until you get a perfect amalgam.
7. Now add the other dry ingredients, and mix it up to get a smooth mixture.
8. Spread an oven plate with the batter that you have gotten, then let it cook for about 12-15 minutes: to make sure of the cooking you can make fences test.
9. Once crush, take the cake out and let it cool.
10. To prepare the frosting, you need to beat butter and honey together up to get a smooth mixture.
11. Gradually add half of powdered sugar with salt, and then mix it all.
12. Now add vanilla and 4 spoons of water or milk, therefore mix it to conform.

13. Once the frosting will be ready, spread it on every side and the surface of the cake, up to make it coloured completely of white.
14. Once completed the coverage, take the black frosting and make a layer of it on the complete surface, without the sides.
15. One it just dries a little, you have you scatter the gummy worms on the cake.

The beautiful Upsidedown vanilla Cake is as good as dreadful. Proof is in the pudding!

Demogorgon Cake

The Upsidedown is a dreadful and wicked place, and the poor Will never stops to fight against the demons who live in there. Demogorgon is one of the appalling beings, and "it doesn't have a face." We wanted to create then a unique recipe, amazing to see and in perfect style Stranger Things, with the strange face of the Demogorgon. We're going to prepare it.

Ingredients (x4 people):
- 200 gs flour
- 100 gs of sugar
- 450 gs of toasted almonds
- 425 gs of pumpkin cream
- 600 gs of cherries
- 300 mls of sweetened condensed milk
- 100 gs of butter
- 3 eggs
- 100 gs of blueberries cream
- 100 gs of flakes almonds
- 5 rolls of puff pastry
- 1 pinch of salt
- ½ water's glass
- Caramel topping

Preparation:
1. Take a big bowl and pour inside the flour, the salt and the butter.
2. Mix it all together with hands until you get a little ball of homogeneous and compact pasta. Lei it rest for 20 minutes.
3. Now take a rolling pin, stretch the pasta, and make it become thin.
4. Take now a tray of deep circular aluminium, position it to the inside, and make it take the form of the container. Now put aside.
5. You turn on the oven to 220°C.
6. Now in another container pour the pumpkin cream, the cherries, two eggs and the milk.
7. With a whip beat well the content for a few minutes up to make amalgamate all ingredients.
8. Pour now the mixture inside the base for the cake, and then insert it in oven for 15 minutes. After that, lower the temperature to 180°C and ley it cook for other 40 minutes.
9. In the meantime, we will go to create the leaves to put in the sides.
10. Take a piece of paper and draw a giant leaf, then cut it out.
11. Stretch the first roll of puff pastry and, with the leaf form cut it out; you go with the box cutter to create a leaf of pasta.
12. Do the same with the others four and you will have five leaves to put in the sides of the cake.
13. Now take a little container and break the egg remained to the inside, then pour water's glass. Mix with a fork.
14. Take a brush from kitchen and smear the egg and the water for ¾ of the surface of every leaf, and later insert us one by one the almonds where you have spreaded the mixture.

15. Introduce them in oven for 15 minutes up to make them become rigid and crisp.
16. When the cake has finished cooking, take it out from the oven and put it in a greater container, always fund, without raising it from the aluminum.
17. Now position the flakes of almonds for the whole surface, and then let it cool.
18. Take the leaves from the oven and insert them to the sides of the cake in vertical position. What we need is to recreate the face of the Demogorgon when it's open.
19. One you've done that, spread caramel topping among the leaves, as it seemed the drivel of the Demogorgone.

Here to you Demogorgon Cake, the most anxious and grisly dessert that you will ever have created, in perfect style Stranger Things. Enjoy your meal!

WAFFLE DOLCI

Strawberry ice cream and candies waffle sandwiches

After Eleven ate a savory hamburger, the she also thrown strawberry ice cream down. Even if she had no problem in replace waffes with hamburgers, we have thought about creating for her a mix of everything, giving life to the Strawberry ice cream and candies waffle sandwiches. Let's see how we can prepare it.

Ingredients (x4 people):
- 150g of flour 0
- 2 teaspoons of yeast powdered
- 1 teaspoon of sugar
- 2 eggs
- 50g of butter
- 100 mls of milk
- Strawberry ice cream
- Candies of crushed ginger

Preparation:
1. According to how many sandwiches you want to prepare, you will need to create the waffles dough.
2. Take two bowls, a small and another bigger. Break the eggs and separate the content, the egg whites in that small and the yolks in the other.

3. Now mount the egg whites and work the yolks instead with the sugar until the clumps will disappear.
4. Make to heat a small pot and put the butter inside to make it melt. When it's done, let it cool.
5. Now pour the butter and the egg whites in the bowl of the yolks and then mix the all with care.
6. Always keeping on working for well the mixture, also add the flour, the yeast, the salt and the milk.
7. Make everything amalgamate well, and when a dense and creamy mixture will have gone out, let it rest.
8. In the meantime, heat the waffle iron until it becomes hot.
9. To this point, pour one by one a small ladle of the mixture, so that to create so many small waffles.
10. When they will be ready, prepare them in a great dish and let them cool.
11. In the meantime, put the correct quantity of ice cream in a bowl, that depends from how many sandwiches you have done (1 spoon of ice cream for sandwich).
12. Add in the bowl the candies of ginger and unite them together, without working it too much, otherwise the ice cream would melt.
13. Spoon after spoon, prepare the ice cream with the candies on the mini-waffles.
14. Once you've done, take the remaining waffles and put them to cover every sandwich.

Your Strawberry ice cream and candies waffle sandwiches is ready to be taste!

Demogorgon Sandwich

We all know by now the appalling Demogorgon. Before it was real only in the imaginations of the four protagonists of Stranger Things, but then it becomes true, and the poor Barb has faced the worse consequences of it. Sees the fury of the bad monster of the Upsidedown, we wanted to create a dessert dedicated to him, it could sweeten him a little bit, you never know. Here is the Demogorgon sandwich.

Ingredients (x3/4 people):
- 100g of flour 0
- 1 teaspoons of yeast powdered
- 1 teaspoon of sugar
- 2 eggs
- 50g of butter
- 100 mls of milk
- 1 pinch of salt
- 50 gs of marshmallow cream
- red food coloring
- 20 gs of Nutella
- 10 gs of slivered almonds

Preparation:
1. You must compose a sandwich; therefore, you will need two waffles of average greatness. Start taking two pots and the eggs.

2. Divide in the containers the egg whites and the yolks.
3. Mount the egg whites, after that add the sugar to the yolks and work for well to get a dense mixture without clumps.
4. Make to now heat a small pot and let the butter melt inside.
5. When it will be completely cool, pour it inside the bowl with the yolks, and then add the egg whites in the same one.
6. Always keeping on mixing for well, one ingredient at a time, add the salt, the flour, the yeast and the milk.
7. Slowly work the mixture but with decision to make it amalgamate well, and then let it rest.
8. In the meantime, take another bowl and poured the marshmallow cream inside, and the even the coloring. With a ladle, make unite the two ingredients continually turning, until you make it become red.
9. Now make the waffle iron heat and pour an half of the mixture in. The waffle will automatically form.
10. When the first one will be ready, lean it on a dish and pour the rest of the mixture in the iron.
11. In the waffle already done, start to spread the cream overall the surface.
12. Now take the second waffle and, in the part of the inside, scatter the Nutella.
13. To this point, position the second waffle on the first one in oblique way and then put the slivered almonds with attention, one to one, so that to make them seem the Demogorgon's teeth.

Our dreadful Demogorgon sandwich is ready. But pay attention, it can eat you too!

Blueberries and peanut butter waffle sandwich

The waffles, as we known by now, they represent the American breakfast for excellence, which gives a push to the day in to begin more positively. Eleven knows this too well, and she would never stop eating them. For a perfect breakfast, however we have thought about an innovative recipe, which combines the peanuts butter and the blueberries to the famous waffles. We are sure that the girl would eat them just in a bite. Let's see how to prepare them.

Ingredients (x4 people):
- 150g of flour 0
- 2 teaspoons of yeast powdered
- 1 teaspoon of sugar
- 2 eggs
- 50g of butter
- 100 mls of milk
- blueberries
- 30 mls of peanuts butter
- 1 pinch of salt

Preparation:
1. First, start preparing the mixture for the waffles. You will need just two of them, considering that our objective is to create a

sandwich, therefore the portions won't be excessive. Double them if you want to do two of them.
2. Take therefore two bowls, a small and a bigger, and break the eggs.
3. The egg whites will go to that small and the yolks with the sugar in the other.
4. Begin to work in decided way the egg whites to make them mount.
5. Mix for well also the yolks to create a dense mixture and to make disappear all the clumps.
6. Now, make to heat a small pot and pour the butter inside to make it melt.
7. When it will be completely liquid, let it cool for well.
8. Now pour the butter in the mixture with the yolks and subsequently also the worked egg whites.
9. Always mixing for well, add the following ingredients one by one: flour, yeast, salt and milk.
10. Work the mixture until you get a homogeneous and dense mixture.
11. To this point, put on the burner the waffle iron make it heat for well.
12. When it will be hot, pour half of the mixture inside to form a waffle.
13. Once the first one will be ready, remove it and pour the remaining of the mixture.
14. Position the first waffle on a dish and start to stuff it.
15. Take therefore a knife and spread well the peanut butter above, then the blueberries.

16. When the second waffle will be ready, pick it up and put it to close the sandwich.
17. Make it to rest for 2 minutes and then taste it.

The Blueberries and peanut butter waffle sandwich is ready to be taste, eat it warm.

Peanut butter and Jam Sandwich

Waffles with peanut butter and jam are certainly one of the favourite American ways to start the day. This is what certainly the stramble girl of Stranger Things thinks; she would spend days tasting these waffles. We're going to prepare a very popular sandwich in the American houses, especially in the years '80. Here is the Peanut butter and jam sandwich.

Ingredients:
- 150g of flour 0
- 2 teaspoons of yeast powdered
- 1 teaspoon of sugar
- 2 eggs
- 70g of butter
- 100 mls of milk
- peanut butter
- Jam of cherries

Preparation:
1. Take a little pot and heat the butter until it melts.
2. Then take the eggs and separate the yolks from the egg whites putting them in two different bowls.
3. Add now the sugar to the yolks and mix without forming clumps.

4. In the meantime, make the egg withes mount helping you with a whip or also with a kneader. If you use this last, hold it to the least one of its power.
5. When the egg whites will be mounted, pour the yolks and the butter in. Mix until the dough will become homogeneous.
6. After that, add flour, yeast, milk and a pinch of salt. Emphatically mix. Let it rest.
7. Preheat the waffle iron and when it will reach the correct temperature, you can pour the dough in.
8. Once ready the first waffle, cook another.
9. In the meantime, take the peanut butter and the jam and spread both on the first waffle.
10. Once ready the other waffle, close the sandwich.

Your super sandwich of Stranger Things is ready, it will give you the correct point to face the job, and it will give you the energy that your children require to go to school. Enjoy your meal!

Rotted fruits Waffles

Waffles don't have preferences, they are particularly versatile, they nearly accept whatever type of fruit, therefore the choice of the gasket must be left to the own preferences and the own imagination. Rotted adjective it is used just as a metaphor to remember the series Stranger Things, but you must use with no doubt seasonal good fruits and then make them some small change.

Ingredients:
- 250 grs flour 00
- 100 grs of sugar
- 1 little envelope of vanillin
- 3 eggs
- 120 grs of butter
- 1 teaspoon of yeast
- 200 mls of milk
- 1 pinch of salt
- Jam of soft fruit
- Strawberries and soft fruit
- Black frosting

Preparation:
1. Helping you with electric whips, climb on to cream butter and sugar.
2. One by one, add vanillin, eggs, salt and yeast with no hurry.

3. Sieve gradually the flour and the milk then, always inside the mixture.
4. Work the dough to eliminate the clumps and to get a homogeneous consistence.
5. Now turn the waffle iron on, to make it heat.
6. Anoint the surface of the plate with melted butter.
7. Pour a ladle of mixture on the plate, therefore close it.
8. Let the waffles cook for 3 or 4 minutes.
9. Now repeat the procedure up to finish the mixture.
10. Put the waffles in dishes and then add jam of soft fruit, strawberries and all the fruits that you prefer. It's not well said the quantity for the fruits, you add according to your pleasure.
11. In order to make now seem your fruits of bad taste and monstrous, you must draw above them with the black frosting.
12. Introduce so the frosting in a sac à poche and form some black dots, of the strips etc. on the strawberries and on the other fruits. If you want, you can also add some mosquito that hums around, but always drawn obviously. Moreover, voilà, the Rotted Fruit Waffles are ready.

Perfect for the night of Halloween and for the birthdays of children who love Stranger Things!

Mud and worms Waffle

Reading the name of this recipe, how can anybody go and taste it? Well, anybody won't, except to a diehard fan of Stranger Things. Because, let's face it, after the terror that we have had of the Demogorgon, we surely do not have to be afraid of some worms. We're going to prepare then the Mud and Worms recipe. Only for the bravest!

Ingredients:
- 50g of flour 0
- 1 teaspoons of yeast powder
- 1/2 teaspoon of sugar
- 1 egg
- 30g of butter
- 50 mls of milk
- 1 pinch of salt
- 1 chocolate pudding
- Mint carbon
- licorice
- long gummy worms

Preparation:
1. First, you need to prepared that only waffle that will serve you as base for yours monstrous dessert. Take then the egg with two different pots. In one you put the egg white and in the other the yolk.

2. Now climb on the egg white and instead in the yolk pour the sugar, and initiate to work it until you see no clumps. In the same moment you put a little vessel on the burner and throw the butter inside to make it melt.
3. To this point, when the butter will melt and cool, pour it inside the container with the yolk and the sugar. Now mix everything with care and later you add the egg white.
4. Always keeping on turning with attention, you must now insert one by one salt, flour, milk and yeast. Keep with calm on working the mixture until it becomes dense and homogeneous. To this point let it rest.
5. In the meantime, take another container and unite the mint carbon with the licorice. With this mixture you will create the scary ground of the world of the Upsidedown, so it must be the most dreadful possible. Work it with a fork until it goes out rubbery and sticky.
6. Now you are ready for the waffle, therefore turn on the iron and let it heat for well. When it will have reached temperature, pour the dough inside so to create a waffle of averages dimensions.
7. Once the waffle will be ready, position it on a dish, then take a knife and smeared the chocolate pudding for the whole surface. Above of it, it will go the carbon with the licorice.
8. Last lacking ingredient? The worms obviously. Position them in the surface so that it seems they're emerging from the mud.

Mud and worms waffle is ready to be eaten, in appalling way, by your children!

Apple cider waffles

The waffles can be prepared in so many ways; you can eat them as they are or you can accompany them with sauce, cream or jam. If you will opt for the addition, you have to try them with apple cider, they are absolutely to taste, even if enough binding to realize. Let's see a good variation of one of the favourite foods of Stranger Things' kids!

Ingredients:
- 125 gs flour 0
- 20 gs of yeast powder
- 10 gs cinnamon
- 5 gs of ginger
- 1 pinch of salt
- 10 gs of cane sugar
- 230 mls of pumpkin
- 300 mls of milk
- 4 eggs, with the yolk separated by the egg white
- 50 gs of melted butter

Cider
- 100 gs of white sugar
- 10 gs of maize starch
- 5 gs cinnamon powder
- 1 glass of apple cider

- 15 mls of lemon juice
- 30 gs of butter

Preparation:

1. Preheat the Waffle iron for a few minutes and anoint it with a thread of oil.
2. Take a bowl and unite the flour, the yeast, the cinnamon, the ginger, the salt and the cane sugar. In a container apart, mix the pumpkin, the milk and the yolks.
3. After that, you must take a last bowl and climb the egg whites on.
4. Now mix the flour mixture and 1/4 of cup of fused butter in the pulp of pumpkin, and continue to work the mixture. Use a whip or a rubber spatula to add and to incorporate and 1/3 of the egg whites in the batter. You also mix gently the part remainder of the egg whites.
5. You are ready to cook the waffle. Put the batter in the iron that you have pre-heated and close it. Ready in 3 minutes.
6. In the meantime, prepare the juice, with the maize starch and the cinnamon in a casserole. Now add the apple cider and lemon juice to the mixture.
7. Cook to middle fire up until the mixture does begin to boil. Make to boil up to when the syrup grows thick. Now remove from the burner and mix it with 2 spoons of butter. Keep on doing that until it melts.

Serve the waffle with the cider, warm. Perfect for an evening in company, even while you are looking at an episode of Stranger Things.

Nuts and Pumpkin Waffles

In the first episode of the second season of Stranger Things, Hopper tells Eleven that waffles do not have to be eaten before dinner, but later. "This is the rule!". However, what if we want to break all the kitchen rules, inventing a dinner based on waffle? Here to you the Nuts and Pumpkin waffle recipe!

Ingredients:
- 280 gs flour
- 250 mls of fresh milk
- 30 gs of cane sugar
- 3 fresh eggs
- 100 gs of butter
- 50 gs of pumpkin cream
- 1 pinch of salt
- 1 teaspoon of powdered sugar
- nuts

Preparation:
1. Take the pumpkin, peel it and cut it in small pieces. Together with a thread of oil, put it in the mixer and beat it all for some seconds. After that, the cream will be ready and you can start to prepare the mixture for the waffle.
2. Take two bowls, you will use them for the eggs. Separate the yolks from the egg whites and set them in the respective containers.

3. To this point, stiffen the egg whites, adding only a pinch of salt. In the meantime, beat the yolks with sugar in the other bowl. Once the mixture will be homogeneous, you add the flour. Pour now the milk to thread, few to time. Now keep on beating.
4. Once reached the correct density, you can add the pumpkin cream to the mixture. Keep on mixing and then add the butter. Mix well and finally add the egg white that you have climbed on in precedence.
5. The mixture of the waffle is complete and you can already cook them in the iron. 3 minutes will be enough and the waffle for the pumpkin will be ready.
6. You immediately will notice a darker colour of the usual one, but don't worry about it, it must be this way. Perfect for the evenings of Halloween or theme parties.
7. Now you only have to decorate with some powdered sugar and some nuts.

Taste them in company, to share an alternative meal and infinitely Strange, as we like it.

Chocolate and banana waffles

It is a very common recipe among the American warm tables, with which it is possible to have a perfect genuine breakfast. We, lovers of Stranger Things, however we want to add us that pinch in more than it will twist the recipe and it will do the difference, making it very savory: the coconut oil. We're going to prepare the Chocolate and banana waffle recipe.

Ingredients:
- 100 gs flour 0
- 1 teaspoons of yeast powder
- 1/2 teaspoon of sugar
- 1 egg
- 30g of butter
- 1 pinch of salt
- 80 mls of milk
- 1 banana
- Coconut oil
- melting chocolate powder

Preparation:
1. Prepare first the mixture to create the waffle. It will only needs one of it, but bug, to compose the base.
2. You take then two pots, a small and a big. In the first one, pour the egg white, and in the other the yolk.

3. Stiffen the egg white and in the meantime, add the sugar to the yolk, and work it well until all the clumps have disappeared.
4. To this point, make to heat a small pot and melt the butter inside. Once it will be liquid, let it cool.
5. Now take the butter and pour it in the bowl of the yolk, and make the same thing with the mounted egg white.
6. Pour in the same container the milk, the flour, the yeast and the salt. One by one and always mixing for well it all. When the mixture will be complete and well worked, leave it to rest.
7. In the meantime, put a pot on the burner and pour coconut oil and chocolate powder inside, always keep on turning.
8. Now cut the banana in slices.
9. Heat the waffle iron and pour the mixture inside all in once, to form only one of it, but big.
10. When the chocolate and the coconut will have become liquid, you have to put the waffle on a dish.
11. To this point, pour the warm chocolate for the whole surface of the waffle, and finally position some banana slices in the centre of it.

Enjoy your meal!

Red Velvet Waffles

Eleven certainly love the waffles, and Hopper knows that when he's hoping to still find her in the wood. We have created so a different recipe, all in style Stranger Things that you can serve for Halloween, from the colour red fire as the human blood that Demogorgon want to eat. Let's see how to realize the Red Velvet Waffles.

Ingredients (x2 people):
- 2 manufactured waffles
- 250 gs flour
- 70 gs of sugar
- 20 gs of yeast
- 20 gs of cocoa powder
- 1 pinch of salt
- 50 mls of buttermilk
- 50 gs of melted butter
- 2 eggs
- 50 gs of vanilla extract
- 1 teaspoon of apple vinegar
- 30 mls of red food coloring
- 50 gs of cheese cream
- 100 gs of milk

Preparation:

1. Start to take a great bowl and to mount cheese and 30 gs of fused (cooled) butter, mixing with care. After that, add 40 gs of sugar and 30 gs of vanilla extract, then the milk. Continue to you work the mixture until it becomes a soft and fluid mixture. Let it all to rest.
2. Take another container and pour the flour, the remaining sugar, the yeast, the cocoa, the buttermilk and the salt inside. Now work for well and leave it to rest.
3. Grab then a third bowl and pour the eggs, the remaining butter, the vinegar and the remaining vanilla inside, then also the food coloring. Work for well and then pour this mixture in the container where you have created the amalgam with the cocoa and the buttermilk. Take now the whip and beat well everything, being careful that all the clumps disappear.
4. To this point, heat the waffle iron and, when it is hot, position three waffles above.
5. When they're ready, raise them from the iron and put them on a dish one above the other.
6. To this point, as if they formed a small cake, spread on the whole surface (both sides and top) the first mixture that you have created, therefore the frosting with a knife. Let it all to dry.
7. When the coverage will seem enough compact, take another knife and smear the amalgam with the red coloring for the whole surface.
8. Leave then to dry, and when it will be ready, cut and serve.

Here we come with Red velvet waffles, a recipe to eat with the whole family, obviously, while you are looking at the show!

Triple-Decker Eggo

A perfect recipe for Eleven, one of the protagonists of Stranger Things. The child cannot live without hamburger, french fries but above all, waffles. With this recipe, you will succeed in making to forget all the adolescent problems to your children, just as it happens to Eleven in the third episode of the second season. The three waffles, one on the other, would make the mouth-watering to whoever.

Ingredients:
- 100 gs flour
- 50 gs of malt powder
- 20 gs of cornmeal
- 20 gs of buttermilk
- 3 gs of baking soda
- 1 pinch of salt
- 10 gs of sugar
- 1 little envelope of yeast
- 100 mls of milk
- 2 eggs
- 2 strawberries
- 1 banana
- blueberries
- whipped cream
- 4 grams vanilla extract

- Peanut butter
- Maple syrup

Preparation:
1. Start sieving the flour, the malt, the cornmeal, the buttermilk, the baking soda, the salt, the sugar and the yeast in a bowl.
2. In the while, make the milk to heat, and when it reaches temperature, pour it in the bowl while mixing.
3. Now add the two eggs you beat the all, until it becomes a dense and homogeneous mixture. Leave it to rest for at least 2 hours.
4. In the meantime, put all the fruits inside the mixer and do the same thing.
5. Take then the whipped cream and add the sugar and the extract of vanilla. Now make mount everything.
6. As it regards the maple syrup, pour it in a pot and add whipped cream and butter. Let it cook for about 10 minutes while mixing.
7. To this point, when the mixture will be ready, pour it all in the waffle iron and divide the dough in three parts.
8. On the dish that you will serve, pour the peanut butter and the maple syrup.
9. Position then the first waffle, and add the beaten fruit and the whipped cream above. After every layer, add the other waffle above and continue this way.
10. Arrived in surface, do a beautiful layer of whipped cream and then add peanut butter and syrup again.

Triple-Decker Eggo is ready to be tasted.

Pumpkin patch waffles

During the second season of Stranger Things, Hopper starts to investigate on the strange events that are making to die all the pumpkins in the fields of Hawkins. For this, we wanted to create a recipe of waffles that will remember a lot those episodes. We're going to prepare Pumpkin patch waffles.

Material
- 250 grs flour 00
- 100 grs of sugar
- 1 little envelope of vanillin
- 3 eggs
- 120 grs of butter
- 1 teaspoon of yeast
- 200 mls of milk
- 1 pinch of salt
- 50 gs pumpkin cream
- Orange fondant
- Black fondant

Preparation:
1. Using the electric whips, climb on together butter and sugar up to get a denser cream.
2. Slowly, one for time gradually add to the mixture vanillin, eggs, salt and yeast.

3. Sieve gently the flour before, the milk then, always adding them to the mixture.
4. You slowly add the pumpkin cream.
5. Keep on working until there will be absence of clumps. The consistence that comes out from there must be entirely homogeneous.
6. Start to make to heat the waffle iron, therefore anoint it with some melted butter, to avoid the mixture remains stuck.
7. Ladle after ladle, one after the other, pour the mixture on the iron, therefore close it: the mixture will expand from itself up to get the waffle typical form.
8. The cooking must not generally overcome the 3 or 4 minutes, but you can also hold of eye the iron and remove once the waffles that these will have reached a certain gilding.
9. Now it just remains to create the pumpkins with the fondant.
10. Take the both of them and unite them together with hands.
11. Create then some little balls to form the pumpkins. Take a brush and slightly push the surface to the centre to compose a small hole.
12. Always with the brush, create vertical grooves on the fondant as those of the pumpkins.
13. After that, with black fondant, create the vertical stems for your pumpkins.
14. With fondant mixed in these two colours, the pumpkins will seem rotted as those of the fields of Hawkins.
15. Now position them above the waffles.

Here to you the Pumpkin patch waffles. Enjoy your meal!!

Pineapple waffles

That is for snack or for breakfast; the waffles represent an easy, fast, and very savory solution. The possibilities of seasoning are nearly endless, also the most unthinkable fruits as the pineapple can make their beautiful figure on the waffles. Moreover, Eleven would certainly know how to appreciate them. We're going to prepare the Pineapple waffles.

Ingredients:
- 250 grs flour 00
- 100 grs of sugar
- 1 little envelope of vanillin
- 3 eggs
- 1 little glass of rum (optional)
- 120 grs of butter
- 1 teaspoon of yeast
- 200 mls of milk
- 1 pinch of salt
- Pineapple in pieces

Preparation:
1. Take the electric whips, and start to climb on butter and flour together. If you do not have the electric whips, you can use a fork, but you must be very fast mixing.

2. One after one, add vanillin, eggs, salt and yeast, doing well attention to amalgamate it all.
3. Now sieve, inside the mixture, the flour before, and then the milk.
4. Add the bits of pineapple to the mixture.
5. Work the dough with the purpose to eliminate every single clump for a homogeneous consistence.
6. Now turn the waffle iron on, and make it heat.
7. Put a pinch of melted butter on the surface of the iron, with the purpose to anoint it, so that nothing will attach.
8. Pour a ladle of mixture on the iron, therefore close it: there is no worries on spread the mixture; it will make it for itself.
9. The ideal waffle cooking time is of maximum 4 minutes, but you are can assure you that they reach the gilding you desire.
10. Continue with the same procedure to exhaust the mixture.

If you want, you can season with soft fruit or any other thing that suggests your imagination. Pineapple waffles represent a savory dessert for the summer, but also a substantial simple breakfast for the one who does not have a lot of time to devote to the stoves. It's perfect over that for all those people which love an Anglo-Saxon touch in the kitchen. Ideal to eat while you are enjoying an episode of Stranger Things!

Christmas lights waffles

Who has not be moved by the episode in which Joyce tries to communicate with his child Will through the lights of Christmas and the alphabet on the wall of house while everybody believed her crazy? We were standing for Joyce, and we want to show it to her with an original and creative recipe inspired to her living room full of lights and hope. We see therefore the recipe of the Christmas lights waffles of Stranger Things.

Ingredients:
- 100g of flour 0
- 1 teaspoon and a half of yeast
- 1/2 teaspoon of sugar
- 1 egg
- 20g of butter
- 50 mls of milk
- 60 mls of cheese cream
- 3 strawberries
- 8 or 10 M&M's
- melting chocolate frosting
- 1 pinch of salt

Preparation:

1. Start preparing obviously the waffles' dough. They will be enough two of them, therefore there is no need to exaggerate with the doses of the ingredients.
2. Start breaking the egg and with attention separated the egg white by the yolk. Then you make to heat a small pot and make to melt the butter inside.
3. In the meantime, take the pot with the egg white and make it mount. Mix the yolk with sugar instead and turn it for well up until the clumps will disappear.
4. To this point, the butter will have finished melting, so turn the burner off and let it cool.
5. Once done, pour the butter in the container with the yolk and the sugar, and then add also the egg white mounted.
6. Make to amalgamate well everything and pour it the yeast, the flour, the milk and the salt. You mix well the all.
7. Start heating the plate for the waffles and when it results hot, pour it above half the mixture servant, to form a waffle. When it is ready, raise it and put in the composed remainder.
8. Once that both the waffles will be ready, you spread above the two surfaces the cheese cream with a knife. Only in one of the two, prepare for the whole surface the bits of strawberry.
9. To this point, put the waffle without the strawberries above the other and, if necessary, you give another trail of cheese cream.
10. Insert now the frosting inside a little sac à poche. With this, you write on surface first a line that must seem the thread of Christmas lights, and then the letters under ABCD. Under to the thread position the M&M's and bottom the chocolates.

Here to you the Christmas lights waffles.

Lemon ice-cream and peanuts waffles

The waffles are a typical dish of the Anglo-Saxon breakfast, but with the addition of the ice cream, it becomes also a good snack or dessert. As the "stramble girl" of Stranger Things would want, they can be eaten in any time of the day, above all if he succeeds in inventing some different recipes. Here we go, we'll see how to prepare the lemon ice-cream and peanuts waffles.

Ingredients:
- 250 grs flour 00
- 100 grs of sugar
- 1 little envelope of vanillin
- 3 eggs
- Lemon ice-cream
- 120 grs of butter
- 1 teaspoon of yeast
- 200 mls of milk
- 1 pinch of salt
- peanuts

Preparation:
1. Take two different bowls and the eggs.
2. In one of them, pour in the egg whites and in the other the yolks with the sugar.

3. Now you make to climb on egg whites and then work for well the yolks up to get a mixture without clumps.
4. In the meantime, turn a pot on and start melting the butter. Turn it off when it is liquid and let it cool.
5. To this point, pour the butter and the egg whites worked in the bowl of the yolks and then work with constancy the dough.
6. Gradually and with attention, you add vanillin, flour, salt, yeast and milk.
7. Work the mixture to get a homogeneous and compact consistence.
8. Turn on the iron waffle, to make it heat.
9. Anoint the surface of the plate with the butter or with the non-stick spray.
10. Pour the equivalent of a ladle of mixture on the iron, therefore close it: the mixture will expand it from itself up to get the typical form.
11. Let the waffles cook for 3 or 4 minutes, or in alternative up to the surface is well gilded.
12. You repeat the procedure up to finish the mixture.
13. Put the waffles on the dishes, and with attention add one little ball at a time of lemon ice-cream. You can position only a little ball, or you can fill the waffle with a great quantity to taste entirely the decisive point that lemon gives to the waffles.
14. Finally add one peanuts sprinkled on the whole surface.

Here's a dessert loved by adults and children, the Waffles with lemon ice cream and peanuts are a genial and unique alternative, different from the whole other desserts. Enjoy it in company!

Strawberry ice cream and rum waffles

A simple and fast recipe, that with the addition of some rum becomes special and unique. This time, this is not for children of Stranger Things to eat, but we are sure that Joyce and Hopper would not hesitate to give it a bite. Here we go; we're going to prepare the Strawberry ice cream and Rum Waffles.

Ingredients:
- 250 grs flour 00
- Sugar (100 gs)
- 1 little envelope of vanillin
- 3 eggs
- 1 little glass of rum
- 120 grs of butter
- 1 teaspoon of yeast
- 200 mls of milk
- 1 pinch of salt
- Strawberry ice cream
- 200 gs whipped cream
- 400 gs strawberries
- 2 spoons lemon juice
- Maple syrup

Preparation:

1. Helping you by the electric whips, mount the butter with the sugar. It is not advisable to use the fork, but if you have to, try to hold a sustained course.
2. Gradually add vanillin, eggs, salt and yeast.
3. Now sieve the flour and then the milk inside the mixture.
4. Work the mixture with the purpose to get a total absence of clumps: the consistence that comes out from there must be entirely homogeneous.
5. Now turn the waffle iron on, to make it heat.
6. Anoint the surface of the iron with melted butter.
7. Pour a ladle of mixture on the iron, therefore close it, so that the mixture can disperse, to get the form typical of the waffles.
8. Now let the waffle cook for about 3 or 4 minutes.
9. Repeat the procedure up to finish the dough.
10. Now wash and cut the strawberries.
11. Season the strawberries with lemon juice and sugar.
12. Make a layer of whipped cream.
13. Put the waffles in the dishes, and then add a little ball of ice cream in the surface.
14. Add now 2 spoons of strawberries with a bit of their juice.
15. Add the whipped cream with a spoon or, if you have it, with the sac à poche.
16. Decorate the waffles with maple syrup, then close them and add another layer of whipped cream.
17. Leave the precious touch at the end. Pour the rum overall the surface.

The dessert is ready to be tasted. Enjoy your meal!

COCKTAIL

Eggo my Eggo

After Hopper forbids Eleven to eat the Eggos Waffle for a week with the purpose to ground her, things started to be difficult between them. The girl becomes so much angry to break the glasses of the house with her desperate cries. We further understand here how much the girl loves the Eggos, but above all she doesn't like to respect the rules. So we have created this unique and ruthless cocktail, in honor of Eleven's temperament and her unbridled passion for waffles. This is the Eggo my Eggo.

Ingredients:
- 50 mls of Bourbon Whisky
- 10 mls of Porto
- 20 mls of maple syrup
- 1 orange slice
- fresh cherries
- 1 mini Eggo Waffle

Preparation:
1. First of all, you let the Eggo Waffle defrost.
2. In this drink the shaker must not be used but we're going to "built it" directly in the glass, in this case we'll use a baloon.
3. Take the glass and pour some ice cubes inside, not too many. 2 or 3 will be fine.

4. Now pour the Bourbon Whisky, the Porto and maple syrup, paying attention to quantity. You must follow the recipe otherwise you risk to undermine taste of the cocktail.
5. Mix gently helping you with a teaspoon.
6. After that, put an orange slice inside to give it a sweet aftertaste.
7. Here we come, the drink is ready. If you want, you can add a splah of soda. If not, leave it as it is. It will be stronger and bitter.
8. Decorate it with a skewer of cherries and then finally position the Eggo Waffle on the edge of the glass.

An alternative version of the cocktail is with warm glass. You can heat the baloon with a burner (the kind you use for the cappuccino) and do not put the ice. If heated, Bourbon and Porto, they will make you feel their true taste. Watch out not to exaggerate, it will be enough to heat the glass for some seconds and not its content. Now enjoy the Eggo my Eggo Cocktail, Cheers!

Upsidedown Cocktail

We certainly agree about the fact that the Upsidedown is an anxious and infernal dimension. Everything about that place is dreadful, and Will, after having succeeded in going out of it, still have to deal with his "visions of the truth". The cocktail that we're going to prepare will certainly be more delicious than that horrible place, but we has studied certain elements that will remind you of it. We prepare then the Upsidedown Cocktail.

Ingredients (x 1 cocktail):
- 45 mls of pure vodka
- 15 mls of cranberry syrup
- 15 mls of lime juice
- 15 mls of Ouzo
- 3-4 fresh blackberries

Preparation:
1. First of all, take a Martini cup and pour some ice cubes insede of it. Let it refresh while you are preparing the cocktail in the shaker. Slowly it will arise an ice halo and the glass will be cool.
2. Now take a shaker and put 2 or 3 blackberries inside. Crush gently the blackberries by helping you with a pestle, then add the lime juice.

3. After that, you have to add some ice (better if crushed) and then pour vodka and every remaining ingredient.
4. Shakerate vigorously for a few seconds.
5. Now remove any residual ice of the Martini cup.
6. Now filter and pour it inside the glass.
7. Decorate it with a skewer of blackberries and berry mixture.

The colors are terryfing, but taste is definitely unique and special. Here is the Upsidedown Cocktail, proof is in the pudding!

Friends don't lie Cocktail

When Eleven asks to Mike what a friend is, one of the first things that the boy says is "Friends don't lie." This sentence will stay engraved in the mind of Eleven for the whole series, and she will say that to Hopper, to burden the lies he said to protect her. We have studied then a cocktail devoted to the pure and true friendship that exists only probably when you have 12-13 years old and you really believe you and best friends can change the world. A transparent, reliable and excellent drink as the taste of the true friendship that ties the boys of Stranger Things. Friends don't lie.

Ingredients:
- 45 mls of whiskey
- 15 mls of egg white
- 10 mls of maple syrup
- 15 mls of lemon juice

Preparation:
1. Take an old fashion glass, pour some ice in and let it cool.
2. Meanwhile, take a shaker and pour whiskey with the 15 mls of egg white in, that correspond dimensions to one egg.
3. Shaker emphatically for 20-25 seconds so that to mix for well the two ingredients.
4. To this point, open the shaker and pour the lemon juice and the maple syrup in. Close again the shake. Do not add ice in

the shaker, in this case you will just need it to amalgamate the ingredients.
5. Take the old fashion glass and eliminate the water in excess caused by the breakup of the ice. You can use otherwise a strainer, it will be enough for you to turn upside-down the glass watching out for not to upset the ice too.
6. Pour the cocktail and decorate it with an orange slice. In this way you will give a beautiful visual effect.

A simple and easy cocktail to prepare. Without lies and without deceptions, exactly as the true friendship should be. Here's to Stranger Things' kids.

Justice for Barb Cocktail

This cocktail is dedicated to one of the characters of Stranger Things that we miss the most, Barb Holland, Nancy's best friend. And also to those episodes of the second season in which the sister of Mike wants to reveal to Barb's parents of the terrible end that the girl has done, while they keep on looking for her hopelessly. Let's go to prepare then all together this cocktail, because we stand with Nancy, and we want now Justice for Barb.

Ingredients:
- 15 mls of Bourbon Whisky
- 15 mls of Apple Brandy or Calvados
- Cane sugar
- 1 slice of orange
- 1 slice of lemon
- 1 cinnamon stick
- 20 mls of hot water

Preparation:
1. Take an old fashion glass and put the slice of orange and the lemon one in there. Possibly cut to dice. Add 2 teaspoons of cane sugar. It is all right to measure it with cafe spoon.
2. Now take a pestle and gently squeeze the citrus fruit. In this way, a kind of mash will come out.

3. After that, add Whiskey and Brandy to the apple. You can also use the Calvados, which has taste of green apple, a very savory and yielded liqueur.
4. Before mixing, add delicately the hot water. 20 mls will be enough.
5. Now mix, you won't need strength and energy. You have only to accompany the cafe spoon.
6. Decorate it with a cinnamon stick; it will give a definite aftertaste.
7. If you want, you can add a lemon washer as decoration and then serve.

While we taste this jewel cocktail, let's think about the sweetness of Barb, and let's hope that Nancy succeeds in redeem her. Justice for Barb!

Stranger Things Cocktail

A strong definite cocktail, whom the taste will burn the throat. This is what we want to create for remember Stranger Things. A whole series that has bewitched us and abducted us; it cause to us the palpitations and the cold sweats. It also made us move quite a lot. This drink will give you all those feelings in every sip. Enjoy the Stranger Things Cocktail.

Ingredients:
- 1 part Kahlua
- 1 part Baileys
- 1 part Grand Marnier
- Grenadine syrup

Preparation:
1. Take a glass type Collins (tall and long) and put two ice cubes in.
2. The cocktail that we're going to prepare is stratified and it will give the optic effect to be separated in more parts. This only if you will add the ingredients in the correct sequence.
3. Start to pour 1 part of Kahlua, it is the first liqueur to put because it results heavier (of consistence) and it will remain abandoned on the fund of the glass.
4. Then you can pour 1 part of Baileys. This liqueur is also very full-bodied, but lighter of the Kahlua and therefore it remains

as soon as above of it. Helping you with a cafe spoon, turn contrarily even so that softly pour the liqueur. Avoid pouring otherwise quickly the ingredients 'cause the cocktail won't stratify.

5. Once formed the first two layers, it just remains the last liqueur: Grand Marnier. Slightly spicy to the orange, it is particularly light and it can remain in the surface of the glass above Kahlua and Baileys.
6. To this point, you will notice the three layers of different colours. From the black to the grey-brown.
7. Add now some drops of grenadine syrup. Not mixing, the cocktail must be drunk as it is. As soon as you drink it, you will feel the different tastes according to the layer. Drink it alone, with the friends, in family or during a party.

It's always time for think about the most beautiful series of the year, with an unique and certainly "Strange" drink in your hand!

Printed in Dunstable, United Kingdom